Lessons from
the Dojo Floor

Lessons from
the Dojo Floor

KRIS WILDER

To order additional copies of this book, contact:
Xlibris Corporation
1-888-795-4274
www.Xlibris.com
Orders@Xlibris.com
18433

Contents

While the lessons I have to share are based in karate and Judo, I believe these lessons and experiences are not exclusive to the martial arts. It is my hope that the reader realizes, sooner in life than I did, that the lessons of this world abound and come from many sources. The lessons are not always found tied around the waist of the instructor.

Thank you to my wife Debra and Lawrence Kane for their help and support.

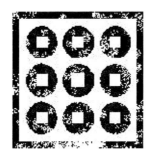

Karate Is More than Stylized Brutality

MANY STUDENTS FIND the rituals of a martial arts school burdensome, consider them worthless at worst, or at best, believe the rituals have little to do with what they came to learn. This opinion changes over time as the student begins to realize that while karate and many similar arts are focused on injuring an attacker, the rituals and the courtesy bring a necessary balance to the art. Without these rituals, karate would be nothing more than stylized brutality. The dojo ethics, morals and codes of conduct are ignored only at the peril and assured detriment of the martial artist.

Looking at the Sunset

I F YOU LOOK at a sunset through a straw, you see the sun's orange, blinding brilliance, a brilliance so overpowering that when you look away, you cannot see anything else. Looking through a straw also makes for a narrow view that fails to see the subtleties that can turn the landscape into a picture more beautiful than any painter can render.

When you begin training, it is like looking at the sunset through a straw. Your view is narrow and fixated on the bright sun, or on the striking, locking, throwing, and your eventual dominance of your opponent. As you train and the straw is lowered from your eye, your vision adjusts to the more subtle lighting, and you begin to see the broader landscape in a new way.

Every novice martial artist begins training by looking through the straw. Some beginners never stick to the training long enough to see the landscape. Many leave because they cannot continue, due to other responsibilities that are more important. But many leave because they never stay long enough to see the beauty of the sunset.

Konstantin Sergeevich Stanislavski

S TANISLAVSKI, A FAMOUS acting instructor and author, said of technique, "The purpose of technique is to feed the talent." The same is true in martial arts. Technique must be the first priority to learn. Once the technique has been learned and absorbed, the expression of the talent can be accomplished through the technique, and the blending of technique and talent become invisible. I cannot think of one person who was serious about becoming an actor and did not take any acting classes. Similarly, to attempt the martial arts without proper instruction condemns the practitioner to failure.

Disciplines and Systems

I N COLLEGE, I trained with a karate club that left me with lifelong friends. When I had to move away, I asked my instructor, Steve Olfs, to recommend a new dojo, where I would be able to train with other members of our system. Instead of answering my question the way I thought he would, he told me to find a good instructor from whom I could learn.

His answer was so simple. I was somewhat alarmed that he did not offer the name of an associated dojo or instructor. He did not mention anything about systems or styles. Twenty years and several instructors later, I now know that he was right. A particular discipline or style is not always the path to a rewarding training experience. This sage advice restrained me from associating with some less than scrupulous individuals and encouraged me to seek high-quality instructors, regardless of style.

Open Door

THERE IS A truism that applies to all martial arts: "Every student is leaving the dojo from the first day they arrive."

Eventually, students leave. Some choose to leave because of changes in their lives, their work, or their family status. Some leave because they have achieved their personal goal, such as increased self-confidence or weight loss. Some are asked to leave, while others simply drift away.

There are as many reasons as there are students. The one constant thing that an instructor can offer is an open door that swings in both directions. All sincere students are welcome, and anyone may leave at any time.

Karate is Not About Unity

O N THE SURFACE, karate may appear to be about unity. To the beginner or casual observer, the students in a martial arts class all move in harmony and in the same sequence, crackling with organization and togetherness. However, karate is about differences. It always has been and always will be. Many people and organizations talk about unification. However, karate differentiates its practitioners from the rest of the world through actions–a combination of mental discipline, stylized brutality, and a standard of ethics.

The attire is different from what other people wear to work out. The language is foreign. The hierarchy of the dojo is unusual in Western culture. So the next time the word "unity" is put forward in a dojo, look around and see what efforts are made to set the group outside of mainstream behavior and those that are conforming in nature. I think you will find more effort placed on separation than on unity.

Little Birds

I HAVE A friend who is a skilled tracker. He frequently goes into the woods to track animals and exercise his skills to see what the forests can tell him. One day, we were walking along a creek and he said, "Listen. Something is going on ahead of us."

Being a rookie at woodsmanship, I asked him how he knew. He told me that the little birds tell you what is going on. They live close to the ground and are attentive to what is happening nearby that could threaten them.

He asked me to stop and listen to them, and I did. I asked him, "What are they saying?" He replied, "I'm not sure, but listen to the clatter they are making. Something is in their territory and they are warning each other about the intruder."

He was right, of course. Once I tuned in to their calls, it was obvious that something was afoot. We continued to walk and listen. As we rounded a corner in the woods, I expected to see other people, or a dog, or something. But there was nothing.

I asked my friend, "Where is the threat that the birds are so worked up about? I don't see anything."

He looked over at me and said, "It's us."

This lesson from my friend, which I felt should have been obvious to me from the start, made me feel rather dense and not particularly insightful or observant. He then pointed to the sky. "See those crows? They are too high and too far away to threaten these birds or to tell us anything about threats to them or to us. The little birds tell you. The big birds don't help you much."

A beginning martial artist often asks unexpected questions on the dojo floor. Do not overlook the nuances of their questions. That simple question, asked by a novice or "little bird," can lead you to examine exactly what you are doing and why.

A Safe Place

I F YOU ASK my sensei, "Who is the worst promotion tester you have ever seen?" he will undoubtedly point his finger at me and say, "He is." It is true. In fact, my test anxiety was so high that during my shodan (black belt) test, I forgot how to count to ten in Japanese, which was one of the first things I had learned many years before.

All that changed one autumn. I was in the dojo of Sensei Marcus Davila from Orlando, Florida. We were standing in his office after a workout and he was talking about his students, how far many had come and some of the challenges that others faced. On the corner of his desk sat an advancement certificate that was dated a week or so previous.

Pointing to the certificate, I asked, "Why hasn't she come back to class to pick that up?"

"Oh, she was here tonight." he responded. "She has to test again."

"Really?" I asked. "I don't get it."

Davila Sensei reached for the certificate, adjusting it with a light touch of his fingers. "She tests very poorly." He paused and went on, "She is capable of better, and I see it every night that she is here, training. But she just falls apart during tests."

So I thought to myself, "She passed, I mean, there sits her certificate."

Davila Sensei sat back in his chair and made a statement about his student that changed the way I would test forever. "You see, my dojo is a safe place, you are among friends here, and there should be no fear. When she can test without fear, she can have her certificate. Until then, it will stay here as an incentive."

I took that lesson and applied it to my next test. Upon finishing my test, my instructor walked up to me, shook my hand and jokingly said, "Do I know you? Because whoever was testing out there wasn't the guy I know."

It was me, however. I had relaxed enough to practice the lesson I learned from Davila Sensei. When I finally realized that I was among friends who encouraged me and shared their skills and knowledge with me, my dojo became a safe haven, where I was able to test without fear.

KRIS WILDER

Teaching styles

I N THE COURSE of some twenty-five years of martial arts training, I have experienced a multitude of instructors and teaching styles. I really have run into the good, the bad, the ugly, and everything in-between. I have tried to take lessons from each of these models, emulating the good examples and striving to do things differently from the bad ones.

When it comes to teaching styles, there are many varieties. The styles run the gamut, from the extremely dominating instructor to the casual, almost health club-style instructor, and through all flavors in-between. Pride is good, tradition is good, respect and discipline are good. However, be wary of instructors that make too much of what they practice. For example, I know an instructor that has "Sensei" written in script across his motorcycle helmet. This same person introduced himself to me with, "I am Sensei 'X,' I have over sixty trophies, you have probably heard of me."

On the other side of the coin, I can recall being at a seminar where the man who ran the video camera was a well-seasoned and respected jiu-jitsu practitioner. I never would have known who this photographer was if someone had not told me.

Both of these men were instructors; one taught martial arts, one fed his ego.

A good instructor uses pride, tradition, respect, and discipline to carefully temper and build good practitioners; a poor instructor uses a teaching style to break people. A good instructor keeps a distance from students; a poor instructor is too close. A good instructor can socialize with students, but only with caution.

As the instructor, the sensei is not a member of the student's family, and never will be. Good instructors do not share private issues that are best kept between families. A good instructor will politely end any conversations initiated by students that may go into such things.

Poor instructors build tight binds that create a faux family-like atmosphere that places them at the head of this would-be family. This is simply wrong. Like a child who matures to adulthood, the student should be allowed and fostered to become his or her own in the world of martial arts.

Behavior

I HAVE HEARD it said that some people change when they achieve a position of authority. I don't believe that is true. I believe that the position of authority allows a person to choose their behavior. In other words, the position didn't change the person; it released them to behave in a chosen manner. The change I am speaking of can be either positive or negative, but unfortunately, it is often negative. Whether as an instructor or a superior in the workplace, we must guard against acting in heady, irresponsible ways; we must be wary and be willing to examine ourselves in the most stringent manner.

The following is a two-thousand-year-old proverb, still quite relevant in modern times: "The soul is dyed the color of its thoughts. Think only of those things that are in line with your principles and can bear the full light of day. The content of your character is your choice. Day by day, what you choose, what you think, and what you do is what you become. Your integrity is your destiny . . . it is the light that guides your way."

Dojo Relationships

A SEXUAL RELATIONSHIP between a student and an instructor is problematic at best and almost always a failure. Those involved in these kinds of relationships always believe that their relationship is "different" and is not headed for a series of problems. They are almost always wrong.

Personal relationships between people in authority and their subordinates are fraught with peril. Public schools, private corporations, and public organizations typically develop draconian policies to ensure that such trusts are not abused. Relationships in the dojo seem, at first glance, to have much less danger. After all, if things don't work out, the student can always leave–their education or livelihood is not at risk. Usually, no one is fired or forced to quit.

There are, however, legal, moral, and ethical considerations to remember when there is an instructor/student liaison or temptation of a liaison. It is impossible to speak to every person and every situation because some such relationships do work. However, they are unique, rare, and very special. Be extremely wary of attempting this kind of relationship.

Priorities

WALLS ARE IMPORTANT when it comes to martial arts. I am friendly with my students and they return the favor. Martial arts can be the backbone of your existence, but it should never be your existence. The dojo should never replace family or work and the responsibilities attached to family and work. If class time gets in the way of your child's baseball game, go to the baseball game. The dojo will still be there later, but the baseball game will not. The dojo is what comes after your other responsibilities. Remember that balance is the key to a rich life and enjoy all of the gifts you have been given.

Thermodynamics

THE LAWS OF thermodynamics dictate that hot flows to cold, not the other way around. Ask anybody who has been swimming in a cold lake or has found himself dressed too lightly for the cold weather.

A bad martial arts school is just like the cold lake or cold breeze: it takes from you and does not warm you. Good martial arts instructors are like our sun. These types of schools warm you and deliver the very nutrients needed for you to grow and become a better martial artist.

Evaluate the quality of students at the school you are considering. If the instructor and the school are not like the sun, nurturing and constant with bursts of brilliance, you may want to reevaluate your efforts and the reason you train at that school.

Admire, Don't Idolize

WE HAVE ALL seen and, in some instances, have been them: students who idolize their instructors. This is, of course, wrong, but it is not unusual to the human experience. When we admire someone, we want to emulate their positive attributes, and we respectfully appreciate what they have accomplished. This type of admiration is a mature emotion.

Idolization is admiration in the extreme. Idolization is immature–it is dangerous and, without exception, results in disappointment. The reason is simple . . . we are human. A person who idolizes another, especially an instructor, is seeking to fill a void within himself. A good instructor will recognize the student's idolatry and will handle the situation appropriately. Idolization should never be fostered. One way to arrest idolization is to give that student increased responsibility, to help them grow within themselves and hopefully realize that they, too, can grow and become better. The instructor that does foster idolization has a void in his/her own life. Nothing good will result from relationships based in idolatry.

Trust and Do

AFTER THIRTY YEARS of glasses or contacts, Lasik eye surgery returned my vision to 20/20. I was not prepared for this miraculous surgery in many ways. For example, I did not know what kind of tools the surgeon was going to use directly on my eye. I knew where the incision would be made, but did not understand the machine used to perform the surgery. I did not understand all the technical aspects of the procedure.

Regardless, when I was told to hold my head still, I did so. When the doctor told me not to take my eyes off of a target, I did not. My eyes and future visual acuity were at stake and I was determined not to do anything that would cause an error. When I was sent home with medications, I used them exactly as directed by my physician.

Because I am not an expert in Lasik surgery, I had to trust the doctor and the others in the office. Prior to making the appointment, I researched the procedure and the surgeon's credentials, but in the end, I really had to trust that he knew what he was doing. If I could not have placed a high level of trust in him, I would have found a different doctor.

My job was to trust the doctor and to do precisely what I was told. I suggest you do the same thing when looking for a martial arts school. Ask questions and expect clear answers. If you cannot get your questions answered to your satisfaction, you should find a new instructor. At some point, you will have to trust your instructor because you will have no experience by which to judge what you are being taught.

Do Not Let A Little Disagreement Harm Your Training

A DISAGREEMENT BETWEEN students or between students and instructors can truly be detrimental to training. I have witnessed small disagreements slowly grow into full-blown battles until the reason for training vanished. Keep your focus on your training. If necessary, deal with problems quickly with few words, and move on. You are not training to form alliances, groups, or to battle over who is best suited to lead, etc. So ignore the little disagreements, don't battle, move away from the problems quickly and forget them. These disagreements are frequently about cliques and have little to do with who you are as an individual.

Be Committed
to Growth

S IMPLY PUT, YOU should grow in your training in some way, everyday. It need not be a great leap or even an epiphany, but continual progress is essential. If you fail to choose growth as your form of change, entropy will be your result. The universe breaks everything down to its lowest element. If you do not believe that entropy is the nature of the universe, go clean your kitchen some morning. In the afternoon, look to see whether the kitchen got cleaner or dirtier.

For example, one of the greatest compliments I have received was from a returning student, who said, "Wow, they sure improved," when seeing his compatriots on the floor. Technical ability, however, is only one measure of growth, but it is the easiest to see of the three abilities used in martial arts: mental, physical and spiritual.

Mistakes

MISTAKES ARE A part of training. Mistakes are a part of the dues that one pays for a full experience in the martial arts. Do not worry about making mistakes. Understand them, but do not dwell on them. Learn and move forward. What you learn from your mistakes is the most important.

On one United States Senate campaign, I had made a serious mistake. When I was called into the office, the campaign manager asked me my version of what had happened. We reviewed the events and instead of dressing me down, he explained aspects of the situation that I had not taken into consideration, and then set me on my way to "Never do that again." The mistake was big, but the lesson was bigger, and I have not repeated that mistake in my professional or my personal life. So when I say don't lose the lesson, I mean I take it with me and apply it everywhere possible, not just in one specific situation.

Training Alone

TRAINING ALONE IS critical to the solid development of a martial artist. When you train on your own, you get the benefit of being in charge. You get to set the agenda, the time, the place, the amount, and the subject matter. This time on your own allows you to explore a critical component of learning; understanding. Training alone makes the art personal, increases your understanding, raises questions, and allows you to be creative. Training alone also allows you to focus on your goal(s) without distraction.

You may want to experiment by training with music. Try training with classical music for a session, then train with some up-tempo music. Examine and feel the different results. Once, while working on a very difficult repetitive drill, I used one song over and over until I was proficient with the drill's pattern. I can now perform the drill without the music, but the music and its rhythm aided me in my learning.

You may also want to try training in silence, or outdoors . . . be creative! However you choose to train, remember that you can experiment until you find a technique that is conducive to your individual learning style. Once you find a technique that works well for you, don't be afraid to try a new technique once in a while.

One of the greatest benefits of training alone is that you get to choose . . . when, how, and why. You are the boss!

Shodan-Nidan

I N THE KARATE system I practice, lower belts are termed kyus, while higher ranks are called dans. There are no external markings on the belt to distinguish rank beyond the first-level black belt. The prefix "sho-" in the Japanese language means "minor," or "smaller." The first dan ranking is intentionally not called Ichi-Dan (number one or first dan). It is called "shodan," literally meaning "least of the dans."

When a student passes to shodan, it is most likely the last time there will be external markings on their belt indicating their rank. From this point on, the training truly becomes personal. Mind you, I am not being critical of other systems that choose to rank in increments. This method is also fine; it has its benefits as well. I am simply presenting a different view of the process.

Leave Your Garbage

T HE DAY HAD been long and difficult. I drove to the dojo, thinking about all I had accomplished at work, how well I had done, and the tasks still facing me. In fact, I did what almost everyone does at one time or another. I made the drive without thinking about it, because I was not there; I was still at work. I pulled into the parking lot, made my way to the dojo floor, and began my pre-class warm-up. But mentally, I was still at work.

My sensei approached me and asked me where I was. I explained the day's events. He listened patiently and waited for me to squeeze the last drop out of the day. He paused and said, "You know this training is your training. You should leave your garbage at the door before you come into the dojo." He continued, "If it is important, it will still be there when you leave. If not, someone will have taken it away for you."

Although I am not always successful, I now practice this technique whenever I go to the dojo. As a result, my training is better . . . it is more focused. I accomplish more, my stress level is down, and much of my garbage disappears. To institutionalize this practice in my dojo, we exercise meditative breathing at the beginning and at the end of each practice session. This technique helps to clear our minds of the day's events and helps us to focus on preparing to learn. The results have been a more focused class as a whole, and out of that focus springs better training and learning.

Do What Comes Naturally

WHEN WE WATCH films of proficient martial artists or see them demonstrate their abilities in person, it appears that their incredible skill comes naturally to them. In reality, it both does and does not.

Even the novice can recognize that these experts perform techniques that seem to be unnatural. However, through rigorous mental and physical practice, these highly skilled martial artists are able to make their technique appear to be second nature to them. Their expertise, however, is not just physical; it is mental as well. The brain waves of a well-trained martial artist actually change more quickly from beta brainwaves to alpha brainwaves that are part of mind/body integration and result in better performance than those with untrained minds. The proficient martial artist can strike an attacker correctly and damage the opponent's bones, while doing no damage to his own. This is an uncommon skill that can only be achieved through rigorous training and simple determination. Through dedication and practice, the martial artist's body and mind are reshaped to make techniques that seem to be unnatural, or even the impossible, natural.

The Answer Is on the Floor

THOSE WHO HAVE the opportunity to train with John Roseberry, a former world-level Judoka and one of the leading proponents of Goju-Ryu karate in America, learn many things. One of his favorite adages is "The answer is on the floor." This is advice that is simple and not complicated. To phrase it another way, "It is in the doing." Go out and do it. It may be difficult, scary or even mundane, but it is still in the doing.

Acknowledge Your Own Ignorance

THERE IS A WELL-KNOWN, oft-quoted maxim about one's teacup being so full that there is no room for additional, new knowledge. This is an appealing way of looking at things and should be remembered.

However, try to approach learning by first acknowledging your own ignorance. If you are honest with yourself and you do this first, you will not even need to bring that teacup to class. Your teacup might not be the right size, let alone the correct shape or structure, for what the instructor has to teach. Welcome the instruction as new, don't compare it or judge it. Just drink in the tea that is poured. You can sort things out to your heart's content later.

You will find that this attitude is very applicable to seminars, demonstrations, and for exploring new disciplines. In fact, I strongly counsel those who find themselves in a new situation to never speak of their past training. If asked, deflect the question. You have a new teacup that may or may not have room.

Acknowledging your own ignorance and not comparing goes a very long way on the dojo floor. Years ago, a couple of martial artists came to the Judo dojo to train with us. They simply would not empty their cups. They spent each class explaining to anyone who would listen about "How that was similar," or "We do that differently." After about two weeks, they left and never returned. I am fairly confident that they left because there was nothing to learn at our dojo. It is my opinion that they did not come to learn in the first place, they came to show.

To Travel the Path Means to Cross the Boundaries

WHEN YOU EARNESTLY set out on the martial path and diligently apply yourself, you will cross many boundaries–boundaries of self-understanding and boundaries of limits, both mental and physical. As each boundary is crossed, a new horizon will appear, different from the one you just crossed. The nature of these boundaries is that early in training, they appear more frequently and are less profound. Later in training, these boundaries and limits appear with less frequency but are far more profound. To cross a boundary, all you need to do is to start out on the path that you have chosen and continue to apply yourself in a deliberate fashion. As you continue on this course, you will be amazed at the often unexpected boundaries that present themselves. Simply accept the challenge and continue to work. Not only will you enjoy the journey, but the results will be worth your efforts.

The Other Side of Fear Is Freedom

C ONQUERING YOUR FEAR means that fear does not own you, nor do you own it. When fear owns you, it prevents you from accomplishing your goals. When you own fear, you use it as a crutch or as a means of gaining attention.

Make no mistake about it, fear can be healthy. People that say they have no fear really do. They are just unwise enough to behave as if they are fearless. I have a friend who that was cocky, smart-mouthed, and showed no fear when it came to confrontations. In fact, he had experienced enough success with his attitude that he showed no fear. Eventually, he got himself into a situation that escalated quickly and resulted in several loggers beating him, leaving him badly injured.

Rational fear is a natural defense, which must be respected. Rational fear means that something bad could happen and should be avoided if possible. For example, if we are balancing on a narrow, rain-slicked tree branch hundreds of feet above the ground during a raging windstorm and we fear we may fall, that fear tells us two rational lessons: Lesson one: We could fall, but have not yet done so. Lesson two: Perhaps it would be a good idea to get out of the tree.

Fear about things over which we cannot control, on the other hand, is dysfunctional. Constantly reacting to our environment lets our environment control us. How many people do you know that have a good or bad day based on the weather or the win-loss record of their favorite sports team? Proactive people only worry about things they can control. By conquering an irrational fear, you are freed from it . . . and the other side of that fear is freedom.

When You Lose, Don't Let the Lesson Be Lost as Well

T HOSE WHO PLACE winning as the ultimate goal in training are almost always unable to learn the lesson a loss teaches. We all have met them, the people in the dojo that must always win during a training session. Instead of working and learning, they are focused on winning. They will use trickery, anger, and when all else fails, they will move to a junior student, whom they can easily defeat.

Practicing and losing against higher-skilled opponents teaches far more than defeating someone whose skills you have already surpassed. For the most part, anything you live through what you learn from is a good thing. In not understanding the lessons of defeat, you cannot really learn or grow.

During one particularly difficult summer, I worked almost exclusively on the Judo mat with an Army veteran, who was six three and weighed in at two hundred and sixty pounds. The only success that I had against him was when he had an off day. I never was able to defeat him. The closest match I ever had with him was in the quarterfinals at a Judo tournament. I lost to him by a quarter of a point and at the end of the match, I was so exhausted that I couldn't get enough air and came close to passing out. As I looked back on the tournament and my training, I realized that training with him was a good experience and I was a far better practitioner for having done so. I was stronger, faster and smarter. I may have lost to him in the tournament, but I didn't lose the lesson: Do your best and always train with someone more accomplished.

Tempering and Tattoos

I N THE PARKING lot of a local coffee shop, I often see a small car with a bumper sticker that advertises a tattoo parlor. While I do not remember the name of the parlor, I do remember their slogan, "Hell, yes, it hurts."

Getting a tattoo is a life transforming experience. The tattoo will, until the day you die, be a subject of conversation. The tattoo is an outward statement to everyone who sees it. A tattoo will change your life, and yes, it hurts. Why shouldn't it?

Some people use Valium or alcohol to ease the pain and anxiety associated with having their body drilled with needles and filled with ink. By using these crutches, however, the event is stolen from them. The process is supposed to be painful, it is supposed to hurt. Those who decide to get a tattoo are on the threshold of a new phase of life, one that will never be the same again. The agony is part of the transformation.

I am not suggesting that one should have a broken leg set without the convenience and wisdom of modern medicine. No one deliberately breaks his or her leg. However, when someone gets a tattoo, the action is intentional. Therefore, if one decides to deliberately change his or her body with a life-altering modification, then one should be willing to withstand the associated pain and undertake the procedure with a resolute and persevering mind.

Why should the dojo be any different? It can also be a life-changing experience.

I am not saying that the dojo should be a masochistic experience, but change is not easy, and is not supposed to be. Entering into martial arts training is a change. Frequently, training is not a joyride and requires perseverance, diligence, and the desire to face difficult, even agonizing situations.

Having the Right Stuff

WORKING FOR SENATOR John McCain on his 2000 presidential bid, I had the opportunity to meet some extraordinary people. One of those who came into our campaign office was a slight, quiet man, no more that one hundred forty pounds. He spoke in unassuming terms and was quite pleasant. Over the course of our conversation, I learned that after being shot down, he spent seven and a half years in various North Vietnam prison camps.

He spoke with a modest vocabulary and was quite pleasant. I asked him for help on the campaign and he gratefully offered it. I was specific in what was needed when he left the office. Not two days later, the phone started ringing with other former Vietnam prisoners of war calling in to offer their assistance to the campaign.

At the end of one of these conversations, the man I was speaking to said, "If 'Jim' (not his real name) says to be somewhere, I'm there." He then added, "That little man who came into your office is the toughest guy you'll ever meet."

I thanked him for his help and hung up the phone. I could not help but be moved by the fact that this slight, soft-spoken grandfather, who had volunteered his help, was considered so highly by his peers. It really comes down to the phrase, "having the right stuff means not needing to display it."

And that is a good, real-life lesson for all martial artists. In keeping with this idea, I chose not to use his real name.

My Pain

P AIN IS A GREAT teacher and a horrible thing to depend on. During a particularly difficult three months of training, I developed a "rug burn" from the constant rubbing of my dogi (uniform) as my training partner moved on me.

Everytime he attacked, I repeated the same response. The clashing of his body and dogi into my dogi and body made a nasty raspberry that eventually started to scab over. But still, I pushed on with the same response.

Every night after practice, I went through the same ritual, a stinging shower followed by a light coat of petroleum jelly in an attempt to keep the burn from getting worse and stinging even more.

Then one night, I worked with a different partner, who was a little taller and a lot stronger. I was sucked into his technique so rapidly that there was no time to respond. I felt no pain . . . the sting wasn't there. Again he attacked, smoothly and powerfully, again no sting. I finally understood what the pain had been telling me. I was responding incorrectly to an attack. I realized that if I received the attack, flowed with it instead of fighting it, I felt no pain and was in a better position to counter my attacker.

If I had listened to my pain three months earlier, I would have never gotten the rug burn. During every class, the pain was telling me I was doing something wrong. Every shower after class underlined my error.

Listen to your body. Listen to the pain and learn from it.

Some People

A S MANY AMERICANS from the WW II generation became older, they said that they had already done their service–they had won wars, faced depressions, endured recessions, and survived social turmoil. Then they retired. Many just stopped living at that time.

I argue that a martial artist doesn't just fade away, that he has an inherent youthfulness to him despite his age. I have met many martial artists that are able to perform feats beyond their years, because they "use it" instead of "lose it." Other benefits happen as well, from being around younger people, kids' classes, and young adults. More importantly, they have grown toward a unity of mind, body and spirit. Segregation of people by age, in this case, or segregation of the body, brings imbalance, and imbalance gives opportunity to problems.

I am able to point to an instance where I met Don Bluming, a famous Judoka and karate practitioner thirty years my senior. He took me to the mat and made me squirm like a kindergarten kid under his techniques. He still took to the dojo floor and even with arthritis and age was able to teach me more lessons than I could remember.

Sanchin

S ANCHIN KATA, A form of moving meditation, is the cornerstone for several Okinawan forms of karate and is central to Goju-Ryu techniques. It dramatically slows everything down to show the nuance of each individual movement, with great hardness and rigidity in strikes, and gentle flow and rhythm in movement. It is a straightforward yet difficult kata, which emphasizes breathing, balance, and perfect body alignment. The breathing cycles in through the nose, rolls around the abdomen and flows back out the mouth. Throughout the kata, breathing is hard, loud, and completely cycles all the air in your lungs.

A student revealed to me that he had a genetic liver disorder that prevented him from practicing his karate at the level he desired. In fact, his illness was so serious that he was soon placed on a liver transplant list. One night at home, he awoke with an internal bleeding and was rushed, unconscious, to the hospital emergency room, where he drifted between life and death for several hours. His body bloated in size and weight by the transfusions of blood and medicines. He spent a week in a coma.

Upon waking, he was told what had happened. To aid in the clearing of his lungs and the healing of his abdomen, he was instructed to do the best he could at breathing. Later that same day, the nurses were called to his room because of a strange sound.

They found him in his hospital gown (with several tubes draped from his arms and nose leading to inverted bags of fluids) practicing Sanchin Kata, the demanding form of moving meditation and deep breathing. The nurses asked him to stop and get back into bed, which he did . . . until they left the room.

He continued to practice Sanchin. After nearly dying and spending a week in a coma, he was released from the hospital only four days later. He returned to work a few days after that and continued to train in each class. Although he was gravely ill and awaiting the liver transplant as of this writing, the disciplines of karate allow him to function at a much higher level than many people who do not live in such challenging circumstances.

Not Defined by
Your Weakest Part

SOME STUDENTS COME to class tired. We train in the evenings and the day has been long. However, I have one student who never seems tired. She is happy to be in the dojo and training. She is not the swiftest, strongest, youngest, or even oldest, yet she is always early, ready to train, and has a great attitude despite her challenge. She has cerebral palsy.

The left side of her body conspires against her will. It is difficult for her to do the stances correctly, and the training exercises do not come with ease. I know she has days when she is tired. I know she has long, hard days like the rest of us, yet her training is, absolutely without a doubt, her own; nothing interferes.

At her first class, she could not do a single push-up. Within a month, she could do seven push-ups and frankly, I see no end to her potential. I suspect that now, she sees no end either.

The Body Does Not Lie

ONE NIGHT, DURING Rondori (free-fighting) practice at the Judo dojo, I asked one of the instructors why he was not participating in that night's sparring. He told me that his back was not feeling well. That particular instructor throws me at will and I knew him well enough that I felt I could joke with him. I teasingly called his fighting spirit into question, saying, "I'm sure you are just ducking me tonight."

His eyes did not leave the action taking place on the mat. "No," he said, "the body doesn't lie." The bottom line is that everybody should listen to their body, listen to what it tells you and remember that it speaks the truth.

Wow 100!

I LAUGHED AT the comment from the white belt in the back of the class, "Wow, we did one hundred kicks!" I laughed, not because it was particularly funny, but because I had often felt the same way. After a conversation with my sensei a few months before, I had learned it did not make any difference how many kicks we did. What made a difference was the one we were doing. From that time on, instead of concentrating on how many kicks or punches we were going to do, I strive to focus on the one move I am doing at that moment.

Avoid a Falling Rock

"**A**VOID A FALLING rock." This is one of my favorite martial arts sayings. It does not tell you to be a coward or to run away. Avoiding a falling rock means eluding or evading situations of potential danger.

Any person in their right mind would avoid a rock falling toward them, yet many people will walk into situations of violence without thinking of the potential danger. Understand that there is a distinction between putting yourself at risk to save another and placing yourself in harm's way because of your ego or a perceived slight. Potential violence is like a falling rock. Avoid it, because just like getting hit with a rock, violence hurts.

New gun owners often feel a sense of invulnerability the first time they strap on a firearm. While most are conscientious, responsible people, some allow this new sense of power to overrule their common sense and will walk through dark alleys or dangerous neighborhoods they would have previously avoided.

Martial arts training can do the same thing to the unwary. Just because you have the potential to survive an attack does not mean that it is a good idea to seek one out.

Violence vs. Art

MARTIAL ARTS ARE many things–internal training, physical fitness, skill and timing, to name a few. Art combines understanding, ability, skill, dexterity, and an ability to communicate the moment to the observer and satisfy the artisan at the same time.

In arts, there are rules of composition that are accepted by the participants. Examples of such rules often found in martial arts tournaments include limited striking areas, weight classes, age brackets, gender segregation, and judges.

Make no mistake about it, violence is not about art. The only rule violence has is to cheat. When faced with violence, the goal is to survive. Violence is about putting your aggressor down and out as fast as possible, with the least amount of damage to yourself.

There is an old adage that says, "When two tigers fight, one dies and one is maimed."

The Cowboy and the Boyfriend

A ROUND 1985, I was in a bar on rodeo weekend in Colville, Washington. All the festivities that go along with the rodeo weekend were in full swing, including the bar hopping that takes place and the scuffles that inevitably go along with it. As I stood at the end of the bar, trying to catch the bartender's attention, something else caught mine.

I watched a very large younger guy leave his girlfriend to go to the restroom. She was alone less than fifteen seconds when a cowboy walked in. No more than five foot six, he may have weighed one hundred and thirty pounds. He walked right over and sat down across from her, smiled broadly and started to talk to her over the loud jukebox. She smiled back and appeared to be polite.

As the six-foot boyfriend returned to his girlfriend's table, a few more words were said and the woman left. The boyfriend then sat down in the seat she had just vacated across from the cowboy and leaned forward as if to talk to him, yell at him, or otherwise warn him away. Everything went downhill from there.

The cowboy responded immediately, since he was prepared and the boyfriend was not. In one explosive move, he pushed the round bar table into the lap of the boyfriend while springing from his seat. In that one second, he climbed up over the tilted table, pinning the boyfriend in place as he hit him four or five times in the face.

As the boyfriend fell to the ground, the cowboy climbed off the table, picked up his hat, and ran out the side door. The cowboy was gone before anybody really knew what had happened or could do anything to stop him.

The boyfriend left the bar with his girlfriend, a black eye, and a bruised ego. Here is a brief postmortem of what he did wrong:

Mistake number one–not letting it go. The issue was resolved but the boyfriend still wanted to pursue it.

Mistake number two–see the hands. The boyfriend could not see the cowboys' hands as he held them under the table and therefore had no warning for what followed. The boyfriend was prepared for talk, while the cowboy was prepared to fight.

Mistake number three–getting too close. When someone gets close, it often means they intend to be violent.

There are many lessons in this story, but when you are faced with potential violence, I want you to remember to ask yourself the following question: "Is this going to be worth it?" Had the boyfriend's ego not overruled his common sense, the confrontation with the cowboy and the resulting violence would not have occurred.

Cats Open Their Eyes When They Are Scared

A GIFTED JIU-JITSU instructor pointed out that cats and most wild animals, when frightened, have a common first reaction—everything opens up, the claws, the eyes, everything, and they assume a ready-to-strike, defensive position. Humans, on the other hand, do just the opposite. We tend to duck and run for cover.

Think about it. Something hits the windshield of your car and you cower instantly. A pan falls to the kitchen floor unexpectedly and you flinch, head crunched in, shoulders lifted, arms to the side. You may think of these human reactions as a tactical disadvantage, but there is another way to view it. If you know another person is going to have these reactions, how can you take advantage of it? If you know you react this way, how can you take advantage?

Worth Fighting For?

I N TODAY'S WORLD, it is popular to not have truth. I often hear from many sources that truth is "relative," or the even more overt "that is your truth." Well, contrary to today's pop culture, there is a single truth, and there are things for which fighting is appropriate. These items worth fighting over, however, are and should remain rare.

Great Achievements Require Great Risks.

H ISTORICALLY, GREAT RISKS have not made the difference in events; however, calculated great risks have. D-Day is an example of a calculated great risk. On the day the invasion was scheduled, the weather was so bad that Eisenhower called off the invasion. The next day, the weather was forecast as only marginally better. If the invasion didn't take place that day, it would have to wait another month for the tides to be right once again.

Eisenhower took the risk, but only after he had consulted the weathermen and the military branches involved. Eisenhower calculated his risk and went ahead with the invasion. We all know how the results changed history.

So great achievements do require great risk, but risks taken only after proper preparation. This is a good thing to remember in competition or in life. A foolish risk will place you in danger and allow your opponent to defeat you. Calculated risk may very well make all the difference.

Natural is
Most Difficult

B EING NATURAL IS very difficult, not only in life but also in the dojo. How many times have you spent hours refining a technique, only to have your instructor reduce it down to the basics? The basics of the techniques are simply natural movement, or a series of natural movements. Not complicated. And that applies to the means of attacking. Remember that no plan, no matter how well thought out, survives contact with the enemy intact. So keep it simple. Be natural.

Sophisticated Defense

I N THE COURSE of business, I had the opportunity to work with a company that was using the biometrics-based technology of fingerprints to allow or deny entrance in secure work areas. I was impressed that every imaginable attack on the system had been taken into consideration. Then the chief executive officer said something that made me think.

"You know," he said, "to breach a security system, it only takes a fraction of what it cost to build it. If you put a billion-dollar communication satellite into orbit, I can bring it down for a penny on the dollar. All I need do is to get a rocket with an inexpensive warhead full of nuts and bolts to explode close to the satellite. Each bolt or nut becomes a bullet, turning your fragile and expensive satellite into garbage."

"Okay," I said, "point made. But you will damage everything even close to the exposition."

"So," he said as he looked over his glasses at me.

The lesson is this. If you think some great magical technique is going to save your bacon, it won't, because most often, the simple will win over the complex. Keep your techniques simple, clean, and direct.

Always Know How You Are Going to Leave Before You Enter

O NE SUMMER, I was flying to a martial arts seminar in the Midwest and boarded the plane a few minutes before my instructor. Sitting near the rear of the plane, I watched as he entered and walked down the aisle, gently tapping the top of each seat as he walked by.

After he got his bag put away and was seated, I ribbed him about having some kind of retentive disorder that made him tap the seats as he went by. He looked at me and said, "If the cabin fills with smoke on an emergency landing, I know how many seats it takes to get to the exits."

I laughed and said, "They have lights on the floor for that."

He just looked over the seat in front of him, taking interest in what the flight attendant was saying and quietly said, "if the plane has failed so badly that we need to make an emergency landing, what makes you think those lights will work?"

Okay, lesson learned; always have an escape route. As a martial artist, it is important that you know your exit from a room, a plane, or even a business venture.

KRIS WILDER

If You Have Moved, You Better Have the Advantage

M Y INSTRUCTOR AT the time, Kevin Ingalls, was watching his class train. After a while, he approached two students working on some light kumite (sparring) and asked one of them, "Why did you move that way?"

"To get out of the way," was the response.

"You did get out of the way," said the instructor, "but where is your advantage?"

Watching this exchange, I had an epiphany. If you move away from an attack and only move to get out of the way, you have merely forestalled that attack. The next attack will come again . . . the same way. If you are going to move, plan your move to put you in a position where you will have an advantage over your opponent.

Your Pain

THERE ARE THREE gradations of pain: mental, physical, and spiritual. Within the physical category, there are neuromuscular and mechanical. In the martial arts, techniques that cause neuromuscular pain are quite popular, but they are also the most dangerous to you. Neuromuscular pain techniques are not particularly dangerous when they are applied to you. However, they are very dangerous when you attempt to apply them to an attacker and fail.

Although humans are built the same way, we are all wired slightly different. Some people are more ticklish than others, some less. Some feel pain sooner than others, while some have pain thresholds that are almost infinite. Because of this, you should never depend on a painful nerve hold to save you in a stress situation–it simply may not work. If the technique does not stop your attacker when you expect it to, the hold becomes dangerous to you because your attacker can blow right through the action you laid on him and blow right through you.

Mechanical pain, such as forcing a shoulder out of joint, hyperextending a knee or breaking a rib is much more dependable.

These forms of mechanical pain also render the limbs less useful, if not useless, and can keep your attacker from continuing an assault on you or a loved one.

"You Got to Turn"

"**Y**OU HAVE GOT to turn!" That is about all I heard from my Judo instructor for months. I had been on the mat for about two years at the time, and that was all the instruction I was getting from him.

What he was telling me was just that, obscure as it sounds. I did need to turn to make my technique work correctly. But in a larger sense, he was telling me that a half-attack would never be successful.

In other words, on the dojo floor and in life, tackle your opportunity boldly and with full technique.

The Transition

T RANSITION IS WHERE advantage is gained or lost. Fighting in the grasp of a hold or fighting an attack after it has been completed is expensive in energy and time and rarely has a positive result for the defender. In martial arts, as well as in life, the time to move or to take action is during the transition from one technique to the next.

You can see this philosophy in almost all sports:

In football: "He was stopped at the line of scrimmage before he could get into his stride."

In basketball: "They never let the play develop."

You get the idea. Look for the transitions, the openings. Those who take advantage of transitions will always defeat those who don't see them.

Nature Kills a Horse from the Ground Up

ALTHOUGH I GREW up on a farm, we never had horses. So when a blacksmith came to shoe some of my employer's horses, I took the time to watch him at his craft. I learned something from that blacksmith that is one of the most fundamental martial arts lessons I have ever learned.

As we talked about the shoeing process, I noticed that he was very particular about how the shoe fit. He said, "Nature kills a horse from the ground up."

After I thought about it for a while, I realized that he was right. Martial artists, I suppose, have died from poor footwork. Imagine a blood-splattered battlefield. A simple slip could put a warrior out of his defensive position and ensure his demise. Strength of technique and the ability to move to attack or defend rely on proper footwork and good balance.

As you practice, learn your footwork and understand it, because nature really does kill from the ground up.

Avenues of Escape

As I WAS working on Nage NoKata with one of my Judo instructors, a diminutive mother of two, she suddenly stopped our movements. She looked at me seriously and said, "Always keep your avenues of escape open." Then she tapped the side of my right foot and swept it into the ankle of my left foot.

"Two for one," she said. Then she demonstrated, in clear detail, how my front and back and also my side-to-side footwork put me at risk of being easily thrown. This was another fundamental lesson that was from the ground up.

Simple Is About Survival, Complicated Is About Something Else

I N A KNIFE-FIGHTING seminar years ago, I learned that if a real knife fighter wants to cut you, he will. He will disguise his movements until the last second and most likely, you will not even see the weapon until you have already been injured. This concept was reinforced by a television show on prison life, where one of the inmates said, "If an inmate wants to stick you, there is nothing you can do about it. Eventually, they will find a way to ambush you." If you look to nature, you see that every animal that has the intent to kill is stealthy, until they strike or are found out.

This concept is pretty simple really. Displays of aggression are designed to ward off attack. A male gorilla may beat his chest and throw grass to make a display of power. This display is much less risky to him physically than a real fight.

In martial arts, when you see a simple, clean technique, realize it is about survival, combat and life or death. Flashy displays of aggression are about something else.

Martial Arts Is Not About Winning, It Is About Not Losing

WHEN A PREDATOR attacks its prey, the predator is focused on what it needs to survive. The prey's concern, however, is about staying alive. Martial arts are about the same thing. Protect, thwart an attack, survive, and do not lose.

Once the predator has determined that it is too risky to continue an attack and that it cannot win, the predator will stop and withdraw. Most laws regarding self-defense are written with this premise in mind. Once the attack has stopped, the defense must stop as well. If not, the tables are turned and the prey becomes the attacker.

Separate from Your Senses

WHEN BLOWS ARE exchanged, the goal is to separate your opponent from his or her senses as quickly as possible. For example, the quickest way to win a boxing match is through a knock-out. When your opponent loses his/her senses early in the match, your chances of injury are limited. Pain can cause you to black out. In fact, I have been hit so hard that I found myself crawling away from the person who hit me like a shot dog. My upper brain was asleep and all I wanted was to get away from the pain before I get more. While some martial arts techniques may be fun and may have great training benefits, remember that when fists come to flesh, use speed and efficiency in your attacks to limit your own chances of injury.

Look to the Past

IN OUR CULTURE, it is common to look to the new, the fresh, and the exciting and to discount the past. For example, the United States space program needed a writing instrument, which was essential for note-taking and for making calculations that could be used in space. Since the lack of gravity keeps ink from flowing to the tip of the ballpoint pen, the U.S. space program was challenged to find a solution to make the ink flow correctly, possibly by pressurizing the ink cartridge.

On the other side of the globe, the Soviet Union faced the same challenge. Instead of looking for a futuristic solution, they looked to the past. When the cosmonauts rocketed into space, they did not carry pens. They carried pencils.

Do not rush to place a higher value on the future. Remember to look to the past for a possible solution or answer to a question. If a kata does not make sense to you, do not discount it, change it, or create a new one to replace it. Research why the kata was created, how it was useful in the past, and how the kata is useful in modern times. With this investment of your interest and time, your martial arts experience will be enriched.

The Spaces between the Musical Notes

MANY PRACTITIONERS OF martial arts perform kata, sometimes called "prearranged sparring," or patterns. But kata is so much more than this brief explanation. Watching a skilled practitioner go through a kata is magical. The more you know about the kata, the more magical the performance becomes. The key to what the kata artist does is what she is doing when she appears to be doing nothing.

Confusing? Think of it this way–in music, a pause or "rest" between the notes provide emphasis to the notes that follow, giving these notes their moment to shine. Without the rhythm and these rests, all the notes would be smashed together, creating an unpleasant stream of noise.

The same concept applies to kata. Mozart said that it is far easier for a musician to play well quickly than to play well slowly. Many people rush through kata in a hurry to show power and speed. What Mozart said about music also applies to kata too. A pause in the kata gives the technique that follows a moment to shine.

Look at your own kata and ask yourself if it is a blur that is unintelligible, or if it is a beautifully composed story of speed, power, technique, and understanding. As you practice, it is important that you take your time. Start with the most basic form you know and slow it down. You will find many areas that need improvement and it will take a while to actually complete each form. Remember to look for the forgotten nuances that one cannot always see at full speed.

The Better You Become

T HE CLOSER ONE is to attaining the desired skill level, the more one sees his imperfection. Some of my senior students assist in teaching the class, usually the beginners. As they are teaching, I watch them do exactly what I did in the past. They try to teach too much to the beginners. The beginners see only the gross movement. Any nuance is lost on them. To attempt to teach a beginner the nuance of a technique is a waste and will result in confusion.

Why is it that these seniors are trying to teach the finer points of a technique? They do this because they are focused on this aspect of their own training. They see all of the imperfections of the beginner's technique. Not only do they want to help the beginner correct these techniques, but they also begin to have a better understanding of the technique, and the desire to refine and polish their own skill grows.

To the beginner, it looks like these seniors have the techniques down. But not so, the polishing of the technique continues. So the more skilled you become, the more you will see your own imperfections, even if these imperfections are not seen by others.

Learn the Rules So You Know How to Break Them Correctly

WHEN I WORK with a truly skilled practitioner of a martial art, I am astounded that he or she will break a rule that I previously learned. The session usually begins with, a "Try it this way" statement that transitions into "Only do this if . . ." and then usually concludes with something like, "Do it the way you were taught."

Usually, copying these artists is a formula for disappointment. You see they have not really moved beyond the rules. They still abide by the rules most of the time, but they simply have learned through trial and error what works for them and, most importantly, how to break the rules correctly.

Imagine it this way–if you remove bricks from one end of a brick wall, the wall will eventually collapse from its own weight. However, if you counterbalance the weight by placing the removed bricks on the other end of the wall, it is possible to counterbalance the wall. This is the place that skilled practitioners operate. They see unusual solutions to situations, in essence breaking the rules and doing it creatively and correctly.

Sap of a Tree

S AP MOVES UP a tree from the roots, through the trunk, to the limbs, and out to the leaves. Think of your technique in the same manner. You must be well rooted before you strike. The more skilled you become, the faster the rooting and the quicker you can strike. A strike without proper rooting may well be effective, appropriate, and even taught. More often than not, in traditional martial arts, however, it is important to first take a careful position, or root, before an effective attack can take place.

Pupa, Caterpillar, Butterfly

W HILE WE ARE amazed when we see a small caterpillar with the capacity to eat every leaf it can find, we are even more amazed when it stops eating and spins its cocoon. Hanging upside down for several days, a transformation takes place and we are in awe when a colorful butterfly emerges. The shift from pupa to caterpillar to butterfly in such a short time is an amazing phenomenon.

A martial artist experiences a similar transformation and is wedded to the same inescapable process of transformation as he or she ages.

A child has more bones than an adult does because the bones fuse with age. A child doubles his height in his first two years. As we age, we grow hair in some places and lose it in others. We lose strength, bone mass, height, and we need less sleep.

Conversely, we hopefully become wiser, gain a greater appreciation of what is truly valuable, and are less likely to act rashly. If you watch the life of a person condensed into a five-minute film, you would find the transformation just as amazing as that of the caterpillar. Our bodies transform in similar dramatic ways, sans the ability to fly, of course, and over a longer time period.

The martial arts encourage our minds and bodies to change in positive ways. Through repetition and hundreds of hours of training, we create new and enhanced patterns in the brain, condition the body, and become something different than when we first walked into the dojo.

Crane's Wings and Human Fists

T HE CRANE IS one of the traditional symbolic animals in martial arts. There are several reasons for this, but for the sake of our discussion, we will focus on the grace and power of the crane's wings.

The crane's wings contain delicate, finger-like bones and small muscles that are used to control everything, from the angle of the wing in flight to the rotation of the feathers. The wings are used for flight, moderating body temperature, shielding the nest, and for fighting.

The human hand is, in many ways, just as delicate. It is able to thread needles, create delicate works of art, and communicate softly with a lover. Human hands can also smash bricks and break bones. An impressive one-quarter of the bones in the human body are found in the hands. Though they cannot let us fly unaided, they can be used to create or to destroy.

Just as the beauty of a crane in flight strikes us, we should appreciate the elegant structure of our hands, marvel at them, and train them, considering their place in our lives.

The Real Story

I N TODAY'S WORLD, we are often asked to make instant decisions: Is something good or bad? Ugly or pretty? Fat or skinny? And so on. Think about the barrage of information, color, and noise that bombards us at an ever-frantic pace. How do we find the truth, or the facts?

My counsel is to be slow in making decisions. Many can be delayed. I do not mean to suggest non-constructive procrastination, but I do suggest that decisions be made only after careful consideration.

First, identify the question or the problem. Then ask yourself these questions: Can it wait? Should it wait? What will the consequences be if a choice is not made right away? More often than not, these decisions begin to come into place with a little thought and a little time.

Students in my dojo often apply this process. When they are unsure of a particular nuance or technique, they wait before asking a question. Instead, they will continue to practice the technique in question and spend time contemplating their questions and the possible answers. If the answer doesn't present itself over time, then they will ask.

This method results in learned ability and critical thinking and will hold a student in good stead for the length of his training.

Out of Anger

MOST MARTIAL ARTS films have a flimsy plot, and I am okay with that. I do not go to these movies for Hitchcock; I am there for right hooks. We all know the plot–guy gets wronged, sets out to make it right and ultimately, a violent justice is served. Although I enjoy this movie genre, it is difficult for me to suspend belief on one issue: the hero frequently acts out of anger, using anger as a motivating force.

Anger means loss of control. Loss of control means he loses, or at least he should in my book. I know that in the world of "chop-socky" flicks, it is a small point to fixate on, but we all know from either real world experience or events in the dojo that it just does not work that way.

Lose your temper and throw you helmet on the football field, lose yardage and get ejected. Threaten someone at work out of anger and lose your job. Beat someone down, even if he had it coming, and you go to jail. In the past, moving from anger has cost me and I am confident that you too can point to times in your life that moving from anger has cost you as well.

Today's Victims

"I WAS EXTREMELY offended."

"I was treated unfairly."

"This is abuse."

"I was assaulted."

Today's victims are spread wide and far. Often, people use "victimization" as a crutch for not dealing with a problem. They define themselves as the victim of some injustice. Injustice and victimization certainly do exist, but allowing every little injustice and affront to live inside your head is destructive and wrong. When these issues live in your head, you are living in the past.

Those who live in the past never grow; their past anger and resentments consume them. For example, when she was young, my grandmother fought with her sister over something, and they have not spoken to each other since then. When asked about what it was they had fought about, my grandmother said she couldn't remember.

Those who live in the future constantly worry about things they cannot control, and lose themselves. It is certainly wise to learn from the past and it is prudent to plan and prepare for the future, but it is healthy to live in the present.

Martial arts are not about living in the past. They are about living in the moment. See the action for what it is; deal with it swiftly, as if responding to a strike, ~~and move on~~. No warrior survived the battlefield by lingering over the body of a fallen opponent.

First Choice Is Usually the Right One

WHEN UNDER STRESS, think about your choice, but not for too long. Your first choice is almost always the right choice. How many times have you stopped in the middle of a new kata and said to yourself, "I should go this way" . . . then think . . . then change your mind . . . then think some more until you are lost and confused?

Do not think too much. Take your first choice. This applies not only in the dojo, but to home and work situations as well. More often than not, your intuitive first choice is the choice that is made with a higher level of clarity before the busy mind becomes cluttered.

Travel East to West, Never North to South

I F YOU TRAVEL to the North Pole, you will eventually get there, and after reaching the North Pole, you are suddenly heading south, an unintended direction. If your goal was to travel north, you have to stop at the North Pole or you will soon be going in the wrong direction.

On the other hand, if I travel to the east and continue, I will always be traveling to the east. The same, of course, applies to the west.

Martial arts are like that. You should set out on the path, but be careful about choosing your destination because when you get there, you are done. Many people set out to become a "black belt" and then quit after achieving their goal, never knowing what is over the next horizon, such as more and better knowledge and depths of self exploration that simply cannot be put into words.

When There Is Doubt, There Is No Doubt

IT IS AN old line, but true. When students say to me, "I am going to be a black belt," I often have a sense that they have made such proclamations before about other things and failed. So I doubt that they will achieve their goal, which means they will not. In other words, when I doubt something, then there is no doubt. It sounds cocky but to be honest, have you seen this yourself? Have you done it yourself?

It applies to other parts of your life. For example, I have learned that I do not need to ask my wife if something is okay to wear, or if my necktie looks good with my suit outfit. If I have doubt, there is no doubt. I just change my clothes to something that I have no doubt about.

The Bluesman Knows When and How

M OST BLUES MUSICIANS do not reach their prime until after the age of forty. One reason is that they have to have "soul" and the only way to get "soul" is through playing the blues every chance they get, every place they can. With this practice, they start to understand that sometimes, less is more, and that simplicity is most important to their music.

Take John Lee Hooker, king of the endless boogie, whose hypnotic grooves are timeless. Clearly, John Lee Hooker is one of the greatest bluesmen of all time. Hooker is famous for laying down simple, three-cord boogie blues.

His style is not based on speed or on the number of notes he plays. It is based on knowing when and how to hit the note. Listen to John Lee Hooker sometime and you will hear the simple elegance that makes up his style. Think about what that has to say to you as a martial artist.

Complete Education Is Well-Rounded Education

J UST AS WE talk about the three "Rs" in education–reading, writing and 'rithmetic–we also have electives that offer us a chance to be well rounded. The greatest swordsman who ever lived, Miyamoto Musashi, told his students to be familiar with all arts. He did not say master them, nor did he suggest that they leave for another style. He simply stated that they needed to be aware, to know what they might be up against. Be sure to broaden your own training, but only after being competent in the three "Rs" of your chosen path.

More Masters, Less Champions

THE WORLD IS filled with masters, grandmasters, Soke, Hanshi, and other such martial arts titles. While this could be arguably good or bad, I think the martial arts world really needs more masters and fewer champions.

Being a champion means competition, and I am all for competition. But at some point, competition becomes less important. The determining factor for this change is age. Champions are usually youthful and at their physical peak. Masters tend to be older and more circumspect.

The biggest difference between champions and masters is that champions are more concerned with winning. Masters are more concerned with not losing. This does not mean that masters cannot apply their trade with efficiency when needed. It simply means that time has the ability to change people.

Wagner

MANY MARTIAL ARTISTS claim to have an exclusive understanding or insight into a particular system. Frequently, we hear or read stories about someone who was bequeathed a dying master's black belt, or someone who was the last to have an extensive conversation with the master just before he died. Regardless of the version, the thrust of the story is always that this person was the exclusive recipient of the last, greatest version of their art's secrets.

The composer, Wagner, reworked several completed pieces of music multiple times. To this day, critics argue about which is the best of Wagner's versions of his work. Clearly, Wagner thought that he could improve on his works, and clearly, people disagree on whether he did or not.

This type of argument will continue as long as people exist. It will rage in the world of martial arts as well, until we have all passed on, and then the next generation will take up the charge.

In the same way a violinist will play Wagner as required by his conductor, I suggest that you do the same when you have the opportunity to be instructed by others. I am not saying you have to adopt what they are teaching; simply enjoy their version while in class. You can choose to discard it later and return to the version you already know. Most likely, you will gain a deeper appreciation of what you know.

Is This Worthy of My Attention?

T HINK ABOUT THE things you do in daily life and ask yourself if they are really worthy of your attention. Do you really need to see reruns of an old television show? Do you really need to work overtime on this task today? Do you really need to go to the boss' barbecue, even though you don't like him? Are the things you fill your mind with valuable–Do they nourish you? Do they help sustain you? Do they make you a better person?

Time is short. Our lives are busy and life spans are limited. If the answer to any of these questions is "no," then you might want to revisit what you are doing and ask yourself the hard question, "Is this worth my attention?" When you ask this question of your martial arts training, what is the answer you receive?

Abuse of the Discipline

T HERE ARE MANY martial artists who talk a hard line about training. Often, these artists will talk about being at the dojo four or five days a week for three hours a night. While this kind of training has its place and is valuable for a short time, your existence, your life, is more important than your martial art.

Your family, your work, and your life should be bigger that the environment of the dojo. Don't get me wrong, I enjoy being on the floor as much as the next person, but it is important not to abuse the discipline by spending all your time at the dojo and ignore other aspects of your life, like faith, family, friends, and work. Do not distort your discipline to serve as a shield to hide from the diverse enjoyment that life should bring.

When You Win, Win Well

GRATUITOUS DISPLAYS AND taunting have no place in the martial arts. So when you win, be pleasant, gracious, and thankful for your victory. People dislike a sore loser and disdain a boisterous winner.

In some professional sports, penalties are now added for taunting, and it is a sad comment that such a penalty needs to be used. When a batter hits a homerun, he trots around the bases because he doesn't have to run, and it gives the crowd a chance to applaud him for his achievement. But the player always displays an underlying courtesy and respect for the other team by not taking too long to bask in his achievement. He doesn't trot too slowly around the bases because that would be gloating, rubbing his achievement into the face of the pitcher and the opposing team.

Winning is important. Winning with class demonstrates character and respect.

Doing What Is Right Is Not Always Easy

DOING THE RIGHT thing is almost always difficult. It is often difficult to quickly admit fault, be direct, and do what must be done. It is easier to not admit fault, to obfuscate, and to procrastinate in the short run, but it never pays off in the end. However, doing what is right means dealing with the problem now so that it will not linger, and will not grow in size. Do not let things go unattended, creating a haze of feelings including guilt and fear. Guilt for not doing the right thing at the time; fear that it will grow, or you will be found out.

Some time ago, I was at a Judo tournament, where a black belt and brown belt were entangled in some ground fighting. The referee stopped the action and sent the Judokas to their marks, and then he signaled for them to continue. To my surprise, the black belt stepped back and bowed, conceding the match.

I asked him later what had happened. He said, "That guy had my arm and I was tapping out. The referee didn't see it, but I felt it, and he had me. Conceding was the right thing to do. He beat me."

That day, the black belt placed third in the tournament, a real third, not a false first. If he had won the match, others would never have known the truth of who really won, but he would know, and that was what truly mattered to him. There is much honor and no guilt in doing the right thing.

Dojo Kun

THE DOJO KUN are precepts or virtues important to karate practitioners. They are often prominently posted and are usually recited either at the opening or the closing of class, depending on the dojo. Dojo Kun are not numbered, as each item is equally important. We sometimes say Itos (meaning first or most important) before each virtue.

Typically, the most senior student in the class recites one line, which is then repeated by the entire class until the progression is ended. Through the practice of karate, the discipline of the body and mind, and the reciting of virtue, we strive to become better people, of higher nature, and better in contact with ourselves. Although Dojo Kun tends to be similar within most schools, the exact wording varies somewhat by instructor and system.

"We Karateka Respect Good Manners"

MANY PEOPLE MIGHT say that courtesy and manners are at a premium today, but really, it has always been that way. Courtesy and manners are, and have always been, valued because they have and are at a premium. Somewhere in the world, somebody is being rude or offending others, and frankly, I have been guilty of being short and rude as well.

Some people would say that martial artists learn and respect good manners because it is the other half of the brutality that we study. I agree and would take it a little further: The application of good manners makes for a complete person. As you look at history, those people that have been brilliant or gifted are remembered and respected. Those who are remembered for their contributions to the world who also displayed good manners are the people that are the most respected in history.

Those people that had brutish manners always have that stigma attached to them when others speak or write of them. Not only do good manners help pave the way for you in life, making your path easier, but those good manners more importantly make the lives of others around you more pleasant.

"We Karateka Learn to Persevere"

"**I**F IT WERE easy, everyone would have a black belt." I suppose that saying has come out of my mouth at least six times a year as we train. It is another way of saying anything worth having is worth working for. It is also a way of saying that the changes that need to happen for a person to come to a certain level of training are not easy, and it takes great resolve to achieve them.

It takes these qualities to live a good life and, in some extreme cases, simply to survive to the next day. Perseverance does not mean taking what comes your way. It means preparing and doing what is smart to push forward to your goal. Perseverance means making a plan to move in a direction and not allowing life to be just a hodgepodge of events strung together. Life should not be lived on your heels, but on your toes.

"We Karateka Give Our Minds to Application"

G OOD CONDUCT AND behavior are essential to a martial artist who deserves the respect of his or her peers and subordinates. Application is the external demonstration of what is in your heart and mind. When we say, "We karateka give our minds to application," we are saying that we will be attentive to what we do and how it affects others and ourselves.

"We Karateka Make Every Effort to Agree Among Heart and Technique"

I F OUR HEART is true, then our technique will be also. That is not saying that the battle will be delivered to the combatant with the purest or the best intentions. Battlefields are littered with the bodies of good men. What it means is that the heart, your emotions, are reconciled with what is about to happen, or is happening.

Knowing your own heart can be the most difficult and challenging task a human can undertake. There is an old and famous story about a Samurai who was sent to execute a man who had committed some crime against the lord of the land. When the Samurai arrived to kill the man, the man spat on his face and the

Samurai turned and left to return another day. When asked why he did not kill the man at that time, the Samurai said that if he had done so, he would have killed out of anger and not out of his duty. This was a Samurai who knew his own heart.

"As Students and Later, Teachers, We Will Follow the Dojo Rules"

WITHOUT RULES, THERE is no order. People would drive on whatever side of the street they choose and employers would pay on the day of their choice (if at all). Following the rules brings a known and accepted order to a process, in this case, the martial arts. In saying this out loud for all others to hear, you are making a public proclamation that you will follow the dojo rules. Should you disagree with the rules and be public about it, you are breaking your word for all to see.

Remember, You Represent the School

WHEN WE LEFT for field trips in grade school, we frequently got some version of "Remember, you represent the school, so be on your best behavior" from our teacher. This is very important in the martial arts as well, because should you or somebody from your school decide that they are going to act in a disreputable way, that incident and the student's name will be forgotten, but the school's name will not. So remember what your grade school teacher told you and honor your dojo, school, or club with your behavior.

White Belts Are the Most Dangerous?

I N MY BUSINESS of public affairs, we often look down our noses at people that construct campaigns designed to persuade the public that are put together by rookies. But sometimes, they succeed through creativity and a lack of understanding that they are doing it the wrong way. They do not know where the pitfalls are or the danger that they have placed their project in, and so they work along, blissfully believing they are doing the right things.

This is what makes novice martial artists so dangerous. They do not know what they are doing and nobody has told them differently. Be extra attentive when working with beginners. Remember–to an expert, there is only one way to do something, while to a beginner, there are many.

Give Instructions on a Positive Note

I HAD AN instructor who would praise privately and criticize publicly. His reasoning was that praise was to be meted out sparingly because the student might get a big head, and criticizing publicly provided the group with a better understanding of what was not acceptable.

I disagree. Sure, there are times that a public chastisement might be appropriate, but only after other private means have failed. If private counseling has failed, you as the instructor may have failed as well. Making your dojo a place where people are nurtured and can grow as martial artists and as people is essential. The rest of the world is tough enough already.

Always Give Something to Work On

T HERE ARE MANY ways to instruct, teach, or coach. One of the best ways is to give a student something to work on. Let them know in what direction their attention should be focused, leave it with them, let them sit with it and work on it. They eventually will learn it and it will be theirs to keep. People internalize and remember what they have figured out for themselves. It is also important to give them something to work on. It keeps the mind continuing in the right direction, forward and learning.

Always Use the Body in Harmony

I AM CONTINUALLY amazed at how I separate my body, only using one arm to move something, or lifting incorrectly. We all do it too, even with the bulletins that are posted in the workplace telling us not to do so. We ignore the good advice of chiropractors, medical doctors, personal trainers, and yes, even our instructors.

The chances of being successful in a Judo throw without using our entire body are slim. The chances of striking with all your power, while not using your entire body, are also slim.

A unified body only comes from being attentive to the details of your body. Everything from how you prefer to sleep, to how you sit at a desk can be a learning experience in how you treat your body and how it responds. When it comes to the dojo floor, work to unify your body–have it work in concert, look to the forms, and look to your instructor to aide you in gaining unified body movement.

As You Age

THE SPIRIT IS what determines the shape of your art. As I age, this statement becomes more profound. When I was in my teens and early twenties, I knew that muscular strength was the key to martial arts success. I was sure of it. Now that I am older, it is clear that it is my spirit.

Am I able to do as many repetitions of a technique as the younger students in the dojo? More often than not, the answer is yes, but not because of superior physical training. Most of the time, by being in the moment, making no assumptions about what is next, and listening to what is being said, I am able to move with a greater economy of movement. That does not mean that I am shorting a technique. What it means is that if I am of a relaxed mind and enjoy what I am doing and learning, then my spirit and my attitude determine the shape of my art for me.

The Highest Rank Is Responsible, Always

PARENTS WILL OFTEN leave the eldest child in charge of younger children. It is the same way in the dojo. If you outrank your partner and he or she is hurt while training, it is your fault. Rarely are there exceptions. You have the training. You control the pace. And you know what is potentially harmful.

A Calm Fist Means a Calm Mind

I N THE WORLD of human physiology, it is difficult, however, not impossible, for a person to have a closed fist and be calm. There is a saying in the martial arts that goes, "If your anger goes first, hold your fist. If your fist goes first, hold your anger."

Recently, in a nearby town, a simple dispute at a tavern escalated to a fight. One of the men involved was killed after being punched only three times. The man who did this was sentenced to seven years in prison. The result was seven years in prison, a grieving widow, and fatherless children, all because of a disagreement. This is certainly not something of which to be proud.

If You Are Not Eligible for the Place You Have Put Yourself

I HAVE SEEN many people who are elevated to positions of power or responsibility for which they were not ready. Ultimately, this is a formula for failure.

Many times, I was confident that I was ready for a position that sat in front of me. I knew I could do a better job, I had a better vision of what needed to be done, and I had more experience. However, for many reasons, I was passed over. Worse yet, others below me were advanced ahead of me.

How could this be? Clearly, it was envy, or I was a threat to them, it had to be something like that. In retrospect, however, the fact was I was ill suited for the position because of my disposition, my ego, or my other faults. At the time, I was angry and resentful. But now that I am older and see what my superiors saw, I think that if I had been placed in one of those positions, I would have failed, and failed quickly.

It is almost certain you will lose your heart if you are not ready for the path you are on. The wrong path can be very seductive. I was blessed by having people in front of me that could see this. I am confident that you could sit down and make a quick list of people in powerful positions that have not just failed, but outright abused their situations. These are people that have been placed in positions they are not ready for, and we can all learn from their mistakes.

If you find yourself passed over for what you see as a deserved promotion, look long and quietly at yourself. Your instructor or employer may see something you need to see.

KRIS WILDER

An Art Cheaply Achieved Is Worthless

I HEARD AN interior designer say one time, "Frame it and it is art." He took five minutes, tore and glued colored tissue paper to a white background, and framed it. "Tada! Art!" he announced.

Let me ask you this, what would he get for that art in a garage sale? Perhaps $5, if he was lucky. The frame and glass certainly cost more than that. The "art" actually drove down the value of the frame.

This is the same in martial arts. Cheaply achieved art is worthless. It can even drive down the value of the expensive uniform it is contained within.

There Is Enough Pressure in the World; You Do Not Need Any More than Necessary in the Dojo

I WAS AT a seminar at the Seattle Jiu-Jitsu Club, talking to a student from another dojo during a break. She told me that she was new to the arts and that she really loved the place where she trained. She was substantially smaller than all of the other students. In fact, she was the only woman—yet she felt no pressure.

She said, "These guys are great, they work me hard but just beyond my ability, not too much." Then she went on to add, "I never think about work or anything else while I am here either."

I knew she was on the right path; she was learning and being challenged, but not being pressured. She was gaining knowledge and enjoying her art.

This was a tribute to the other people in the dojo as much as it was to her. She had set out on a path with the right people. She was happy to let them drive the training because she trusted them to do the right thing by her, and they trusted her to put her best effort forward. The three most important ingredients to a great dojo were being demonstrated on an ongoing basis. She will do well.

He Searches for Something

I HAD A young man come to my dojo, where he trained for a while and then left. During his time at my dojo, I found out that he had worked with many teachers, and dabbled with many different styles. After he left, I trained at a friend's dojo and there was my former student (really, he was everybody's former student), training away.

It is clear that he is searching for something but he lacks the discipline to truly look into himself and find out what it is he is searching for. Until he decides to look into himself and on why he does what he does, he will never achieve any level of proficiency. Of course I mean technical proficiency, but what comes with the tempering of technical ability comes an understanding of who you are. The path he is on will never allow him to see himself because he searches for something, but cannot see what it is for himself.

People Will Always Turn to the Message They Want to Hear

PEOPLE WILL ALWAYS turn to the answer they want. People marry what they desire–a strong personality, a good provider, a loving mother. They work for those companies that satisfy their most important concerns, such as money, title, hours of work or product, etc.

Many people, however, will settle for half of what they desire and need rather than make the extra effort necessary to gain their real prize. A strange situation when you break it down because they are saying, "I need this, but I will settle for a lesser version of it." Sounds sad when you hear the words, yet for many of us, our actions can say that to the world every day.

Technique Needs to Be Invisible

WHEN YOU WATCH a truly great actor, he will take you away with the moment that he is representing. To take you away, to make the moment believable, he must help you suspend your disbelief. The situation is not real, yet what he is portraying is real to the audience in an emotional sense. A great actor must convey this without showing his technique. If he shows the technique, he is placing it between you and the experience of the moment. It becomes awkward and unbelievable.

Martial arts technique needs to be the same. It should sweep all things into the moment and the technique should be, well, less than visible. Technique should be a seamless expression of the moment that is difficult to break down to its elements.

That Is When I Feel Sorry for Those that Don't Train

O FTEN WHEN I am leaving the dojo, I am so joyful over the training experience that I truly feel sorry for those that never get a chance to experience what martial arts can bring to their life. The sense of belonging, of accomplishment and fellowship are profound and deep. The entire martial arts experience, from the learning of a new lesson to the tired feeling of achievement, no matter how small, has broadened and deepened my life in ways that are hard to express.

Of course, many people find such joy in other things. One of my neighbors is a mountain climber who experiences the exhilaration of conquering a new peak. Another neighbor shares the joy of music by teaching what he loves.

There are the others, however, who cannot, or choose not, to find their joy in life. It is these people that I feel truly sorry for. So if you have found your joy, continue to pursue it. If you have not found your joy–go get it.

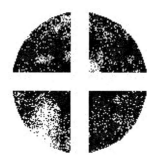

Train for Combat, Practice Peace

I T IS REALLY that simple. By practicing peace, you work to insure that you may never need to come to a physical confrontation, and by training for combat, you are prepared for violence if it should ever happen. This may seem paradoxical, but in training for combat or violence, you come to understand what it is, how it can affect not just you and your opponent, but also the far-reaching result of your actions.

A life can change with one strike. I recall a high school wrestler who was upset with the call the referee made, so he blindsided him with a head butt to the temple. It knocked the referee out cold on the mat.

The result of this single, rash act of violence was a wrestler who was charged, tried, found guilty, and punished by the courts. He was also banned from wrestling ever again. The referee still suffers from the results of the blow and will never be 100 percent. I would argue the wrestler trained for man-to-man combat and never learned to practice peace or, for that matter, respect.

What Is the Song of Your Dojo?

I N MY BUSINESS, there is often talk of corporate culture. Another way to describe culture of an enterprise is the "song" of that business. Is it a culture that allows only white shirts and suits for men, skirts for women, and would never dream of allowing a casual-dress day, as a Seattle-based insurance company once had? Or is it a culture of a college campus, with no real set hours of work, no dress code, and a strict recycling policy? While opposites, were both these organizations successful? Absolutely. They are national leaders in their chosen industries. Located mere miles apart geographically, they are on different planets when it comes to their corporate culture.

So the question is, what is the song of your dojo? Is it one of white uniforms and strict policies, or is it one of multicolored uniforms, where creativity is rewarded. Is either one wrong? No. There is room for both these cultures along with all the ranges in between. It is important, however, that you ask yourself, "What is the song of my dojo, or school?" In doing such an analysis, you will find out a lot about yourself, who you choose to associate with, and why.

Different Is Not Necessarily Better

W HEN IT COMES to techniques, different is not always better. Some techniques work very well for big people, while others work better for small people. Some require greater finesse and flexibility, while others rely more on physical strength. Techniques may be selected to augment your strengths or modified to work around your physical limitations. Knowing why the techniques work is what is truly critical.

To blindly say, "This is the way Sensei 'So and So' did it, so that is the best way" may not always be correct. What I am suggesting is that a technique needs to have everything in alignment, such as weight distribution, rotation, quickness, power, and so on. Those items generally stay intact, yet they can change in emphasis because of height, weight, or injury to either party involved in a conflict. Challenge yourself in what you see in your own training and come to understand why you are doing what you are doing.

A word of caution; however, do not be arrogant enough to assume you can change some technique because it does not make sense to you. It may very well mean that you have not opened your eyes wide enough yet.

When You Stop, You Die

I HAVE FRIEND who is facing retirement for a company where he has been employed for some thirty-odd years. He has expressed some real uncertainties about it. In discussing his situation, an interesting consideration is the life expectancy of the people from his job description post-retirement. These workers only live an average of three years after they leave the company. That is a really sad comment on their existence, but it also shows that when you stop, you die. For the most part, these people had nothing meaningful in their lives beyond their work. Their sense of self was wrapped in their job description, and with no outside passion, I would assert that they really had nothing else to live for.

Martial artists may retire from competition, or back off on the hours they spend, but the ritual and the rewards of training are not lost on elderly practitioners, as many are able to perform at levels far younger than their chronological age. The underlying reason these martial artists are able to perform beyond normal levels lies deeper than their physical conditioning. It is a whole package of exercise, challenge, new people, new venues, and mental challenges.

Look at the great painters of history. To my knowledge, not a single one just quit one day without replacing his passion with a new one. So if you ask me, retirement equals death not because of what the actuarial tables say, but because of what history teaches us. When you stop, you die.

Do Not Challenge the Idea, Challenge Yourself

I N THE WESTERN world, we are taught from the beginning to challenge the idea. We have seen the cowboys who packed up their bedrolls and headed for the next roundup when things didn't work out the way they wanted, or the mountain men of the West who held themselves apart from society, or the rogue cops of the movies who reach beyond the law in the name of justice. The lesson we have seen is that you get ahead by breaking the rules, by "thinking outside the box."

All of that is fine and it has its place. Before you blindly challenge the idea, however, challenge yourself to understand what is being taught to you. When you think you have got it, go back and check it again. Challenge yourself first. Be clear and firm with yourself before you discard an idea, technique or precept that you have been taught.

Occum's Razor:
William of Occum
(1285-1349)

O CCUM'S RAZOR IS a logical principle proposed by William of Occum, a famous logician and philosopher of the fourteenth century. His principle stated that Pluralitas non est ponenda sine necessitate, which is translated as "Entities should not be multiplied unnecessarily." Over the years, mathematicians, philosophers and scientists have adopted and revised this statement to mean: "When you have two competing theories which make the exact same predictions, the simpler one is usually better." Or more succinctly, "the simplest explanation is usually right."

This is a great maxim for martial artists, especially when they are involved in some of the more difficult-to-explain aspects of the martial arts such as Ki, pressure point activation, and other such endeavors.

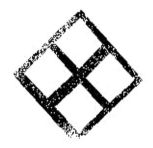

Grow Oaks,
Not Dandelions

D ANDELIONS ARE ANNOYING, yet they grow fast and are hard to kill, as we all know from battling them every spring, summer and fall. Oak trees, on the other hand, are much more desirable. Their benefits are easy to name and numerous. While karate students can be oak trees or dandelions, this analogy makes it clear which is most valuable.

Oak takes years to grow, while dandelions take only a few days. When a dandelion dies, it leaves very little behind. After an oak tree dies, it leaves behind real substance, which may be used to create useful things, such as firewood for warmth, or materials to build furniture, housing, or bo staffs for practicing the martial arts. Whether you are a student or a teacher, you should strive to be more like an oak tree and less like a dandelion.

Be a Scientist–
Have an Open Mind

OFTEN, I SEE techniques demonstrated by other martial artists that have a distinctly different take than I know. Sometimes I catch myself dismissing their example of what is taking place by thinking, "Oh, that's wrong," or "This is stupid." I think like this, and if we are honest with ourselves, we have such thoughts occasionally. When I find myself doing this, however, I make an extra effort to stop that thought process and make a point to listen to what is being said or demonstrated. I have usually been better for doing so.

The worst thing a scientist can do is to presume that he knows what the outcome of an experiment is going to be before he conducts it. A scientist must have an open mind and not make assumptions about the outcome. Of course he is testing for something, but he cannot guess at the outcome. The same needs to be applied when you cross-train in another system. Be a scientist–ask questions, probe, be inquisitive, have an open mind.

A Teacher's Attention Goes to Those Who Take It seriously

A S A STUDENT, you can ensure that you will receive the best instruction you can by taking what you do seriously. Your instructor will appreciate it and you will be rewarded, not because it is some secret code of instruction, but because it is human nature. Turnover among martial arts students is generally quite high as people lose interest, gain other interests, or find that their work or personal life interfere with their training. Instructors will naturally favor those who demonstrate commitment and devotion to their art.

You do not have to be the most athletic, the most talented, or even the best looking. Heart and commitment are the rarest of commodities and the ones that any martial arts instructor is happy to see.

Be Creative

D RESSED IN MY white gi, with a black belt tied around my waist, I was walking toward the gym at a YMCA, where I used to teach karate. As I passed the basketball court, I heard yelling, swearing, and challenging, as did the small crowd of people standing in front of the safety glass that overlooks the court. Everyone's attention was fixed on about a dozen big kids, sixteen or eighteen-year-olds, who looked like they were getting ready to fight. The situation was rapidly getting ugly, almost certainly about to become violent. As I stood behind the glass watching, a voice beside me suggested that "somebody" should do something.

I remember thinking to myself, "Hey, if those idiots are going to fight, I am going to watch and get a free, painless lesson in the dynamics of a group brawl." Then I realized that the crowd was looking at me, the "big, bad black belt," expecting that I would do something to stop the fight.

I thought for a moment about what I should do. I could do nothing, letting someone else take charge and watch the boys get hurt. I could wade into the fray and do my best Bruce Lee imitation, perhaps stopping the fight, but pretty much ensuring that several people would be hurt, likely including me. After all, in real life, even Bruce Lee could not defeat a dozen opponents at once. Or I could think of something unexpected, some creative solution to end the problem without violence or injury to anyone.

I walked over to the gym door, pulled it open, and stepped inside. I looked over at the kids, who had started pushing and shoving each other, and yelled "Hey!" as loud as I could. The guys slowed their tussle and looked over at me, standing there with my white gi, sandals, and a black belt tied around my waist.

I said loudly and with authority, "The guys at the front desk just called the cops," motioning over my shoulder with a thumb. "Thought you ought to know."

I walked out past the crowd and around the corner to the mat room, where my class was waiting. Later that night, I asked the desk manager how the fight got settled. He said that thinking somebody really had called the cops, all the kids had left in a hurry. No one was hurt. A little creativity well applied went a long way that evening.

All Things Have Their Time

A S I WALKED into the Judo tournament, a referee greeted me. I remembered him since we had fought many times in the past. Now, at forty-one years of age, I was still carrying a duffel bag with my gi, and he was a referee.

Halfway through the second match of the day, I felt something tear in my back, but the match was on and I was not about to give up and quit. After winning the match and bowing off the mat, I felt my back muscles begin to spasm. By the time I made it to the doctor, I was on my knees, trying to find a way to get comfortable because each breath made my muscle cramp worse. I could hardly breathe.

After some attention from the doctor and ice from my instructor, the competitor I had just fought came over to see how I was doing. After a brief conversation, he said that he was twenty-one. A couple of friends standing nearby knew that I was twenty years older than the kid I had just fought. One of them chimed in, "Jeez, Wilder, you could be his dad!"

That night, as I lay in bed with frozen peas on my back, my five-year-old son came in to watch the baseball game with me. After getting his place all squared away next to me, he slowly ran his fingers above my ear several times and said, "Daddy, you have white hair." It was clear to me that my time in competitive Judo was done. The message had been received.

I told this story to a Judo friend of mine, Bob Wittauer, who without missing a beat, said, "Great, you can help me with coaching. Don't forget to black out the end of September for my tournament." Now it is that time.

Magic and Martial Arts

CENTURIES AGO, INFORMATION on style and technique was passed on from master to student using oral tradition. Very little was written down, partially because literacy was quite rare outside the nobility and certain privileged merchant classes. These instructors imbedded their unique fighting systems within their kata, which became fault-tolerant methods for ensuring that techniques could consistently be taught and understood over the generations. These kata also disguised applications of the various martial techniques so that outsiders would not readily understand them. As students learned the basics and gained their instructor's confidence, they would be initiated into the secrets of his system. For most, martial arts was an unknown mystery, a thing of legends and lore.

With modern technology, however, the learning of martial arts became far different. Systems have been codified and recorded through books, magazines, videos, and DVDs. People openly discuss the "secrets" of martial arts over the phone and through e-mail. All of this communication not only takes the mystery away, but also makes martial arts accessible to anyone who is willing to pay. All this accessibility sounds great, but like most things in life, there is a catch. Martial arts really are just like magic.

If you really want to learn magic, you can go to a magic store and buy the illusion you are looking to perform. You can read books or watch TV documentaries, or rent videos to learn how master magicians astounded their audiences through the ages. You can even sign up for lessons. However, getting off the couch and doing it is the key, just as it is with martial arts.

Just because martial arts are out there and easy to get to does not mean that people will take advantage of the opportunity to learn them or ever learn them well. Often I find it interesting that martial artists will talk of their wish that more people could or would enjoy what they get out of martial arts, yet lament the secrets being given away. I have no problem with more people gaining access to more knowledge because martial arts, just like magic, can be very embarrassing if not practiced, practiced, and practiced some more.

Have Patience and Have Timing

P ATIENCE AND TIMING are at the very core of a good martial arts tactician. Force a technique too much and you overextend yourself, telegraphing your intent and showing your opponent just how badly you want it. Miss your opportunity and it may not pass your way again. One of the greatest lessons I ever learned in the martial arts was wait and have patience. When the time comes, as it always does, you must seize the opportunity.

I am far from perfect in application, but from long experience, I can tell you with certainty that when I have patience and timing, I am much more difficult to defeat. This is also applicable in life outside the dojo as well, but you knew that already.

North Pole Must Have South Pole

I F THE SOUTH Pole did not exist, then the North Pole would not exist; it would be something different. Often, things are defined by what is their opposite. Frequently, a martial art is defined in the same way, not by what it is in and of itself, but by what it is compared to some other art.

An example of this is my cousin, a Tai Chi practitioner, who gets thrown around most Saturdays by a guy he calls, "The Humble-izer." If an untrained person watches Tai Chi, they have difficulty seeing the martial aspects of the art. Frequently, Tai Chi is categorized as a system that is good exercise for seniors because of its slow movements and low stress to the body. With enough practice, however, these slow, low-stress techniques can be executed with lethal quickness and power.

Tae Kwon Do has been called a sport with no real street application, Judo a sport with all of the dangerous techniques removed, aikido a nice dance that will not work in a stress situation. Every one of these generalizations is wrong because it is a forced comparison with another system, even if it is never spoken. So try to enjoy the arts for what they are and find the one that is right for you.

There are only a limited number of ways the human body can move. Pressure points and vital areas are the same for every individual. Consequently, there are only a limited number of possible techniques in all the martial arts. Given these limitations, emphasis, application, and style really do vary with each martial art. Each is different, offering a unique perspective. Do not worry about what they are compared to other systems; worry about what works for you.

Most Extreme Element

E VERY ORGANIZATION IS defined by its most extreme element. Whether it is a political party or a sports team, the most extreme element or individual is the focal point for public opinion. That is not always good. Usually the focus is on the bad element, the rebel, the dirty player, and the troublemaker.

Even the best of people has an off day now and then. When a star player refuses to sign an autograph or make a less-than-wise comment to the press and gets caught, many times they are defined by that moment. As the famous saying goes, good news really doesn't sell newspapers.

George Wallace, the former governor of Alabama, stood in the doorway of the University of Alabama to prevent African American students from attending in 1963. Later in life, he recanted and publicly stated that he was wrong to do so. But that grainy, black-and-white news footage of him standing in that doorway has been replayed over and over again.

His initial extreme position has outlived him, and will continue to do so. So as you look at groups of martial artists, many of whom are eccentric, remember they may well be the most extreme of their organization. Make your judgments accordingly.

Compounding

C ompounding is a critical element in martial arts. As compounding interest can turn a small investment in a princely sum, compounding can create a devastating martial arts technique. As we know, action is quicker than reaction. Once you have gotten a reaction, you need to compound that reaction by not letting your opponent regain his equilibrium.

Like a building swaying in an earthquake, every effort then compounds the loss of equilibrium your opponent will experience, until he finally gives way. Look to compounding to gain and keep advantage.

Yoga and the Weight Room

HAVING TAUGHT KARATE at a YMCA for about nine years, I made a habit of watching the people around me. On one side of the hallway was the weight room, on the other, an open gym often used for yoga. Time after time, the same scene was repeated. On one side of the hall, I could watch a buff group of young people, mostly men, banging out reps on the weights, grunting, and drinking their protein supplements in an effort to gain more muscle. On the other side of the hall, a slightly built group of men and women were sitting on mats, tying themselves in knots in an attempt to become flexible.

One day, a student of mine who is a massage therapist came and stood next to me while I watched. I told him about my observation and he put it in one simple phrase. "Those people in here ought to be in there, while those people in there ought to be in here." He was right.

While the muscle-bound guys lacked suppleness, the yoga people lacked strength. Good martial artists need to balance strength with flexibility. I try to take that lesson to heart, paying more attention to the balance I give to my training now than I did in the past.

River and Incense

What do a river and incense have in common? They are both going in one direction. If the river runs into a boulder, it goes around but continues on its path to the sea. If a breeze disturbs a stream of smoke from burning incense, it wiggles around, and then sets back onto its path one again. Your pursuit of martial arts should be the same. Keep your direction and roll with the events that come your way. Just like the river or the incense, you need to keep your direction.